MANCHESTER ILLUMINATED

MIKE HEATH

HALSGROVE

First published in Great Britain in 2009

British Library Cataloguing-in-Publication Data
A CIP record for this title is available from the British Library

ISBN 978 1 84114 903 5

HALSGROVE
Halsgrove House,
Ryelands Industrial Estate,
Bagley Road, Wellington, Somerset TA21 9PZ
Tel: 01823 653777 Fax: 01823 216796
email: sales@halsgrove.com

Part of the Halsgrove group of companies
Information on all Halsgrove titles is available at: www.halsgrove.com

Printed and bound by Grafiche Flaminia, Italy

Introduction

The regeneration of Manchester has produced a dramatic cityscape where the futuristic design and imaginative shapes of today's architecture stand shoulder to shoulder with the monuments of the industrial past.

The city has a fascinating history. Whilst its roots are firmly based in Roman times it was the Industrial Revolution that put it on the map and the textile industry in particular that transformed it into one of England's leading industrial giants. The wealth created allowed the nineteenth-century cotton manufacturers to build grand monuments to reflect their success. Pride of place must go to the neo-Gothic Town Hall that towers above Albert Square and the near-by elegantly designed circular Central Library, the largest municipal library in the world.

These buildings, along with the magnificent cathedral, continue serving the community as originally intended whereas many others have been restored and refurbished to perform new roles. The former Refuge Assurance Building in Oxford Road, for so long a landmark of the city with its 220 feet high tower is now the Palace Hotel. Around the cathedral the 'Millennium Quarter' blends the modern with the historical. The stunning Urbis Centre represents cutting edge twenty-first century architectural design and sits neatly alongside the classic 1897 built Corn Exchange, reborn as the Triangle renowned for its fashion shops. Opposite both, in a vast former newspaper printing complex, is the Printworks with its bars, restaurants and cinema; and across Exchange Square is the Arndale shopping mall which, when first completed in 1979, was Europe's largest enclosed shopping centre. This building suffered most from the IRA bomb in 1996 but was rebuilt and improved and has more recently had its exterior completely renovated.

Elsewhere in the city a Chinatown has emerged giving a new lease of life to dilapidated warehouses around Charlotte Street, and on the banks of the Rochdale Canal along Canal Street the gay community have created one of the most flamboyant nightlife destinations in the North West with its continental style café culture, the bars and restaurants having tables and chairs out on the street.

Beyond the city centre lies Salford Quays, an ultra modern business, cultural and residential district that has revived the former Manchester Docks area beyond recognition and is about to unveil the UK's first Media City.

Everyday thousands of people flock into this city to work or shop or both and by evening they have returned to their homes little realising what they are missing. For as the sun goes down the lights come on and, for me, the city is revealed at its most striking.

The buildings and monuments that are eye catching by day become spectacular by night as external lighting emphasises the detail of the Victorian architecture and complements that from within the twenty-first-century structures which illuminates the sky. The bright neon signs that denote the nightclubs, bars and restaurants stand out against the darkness. Wet roads and paving reflect colours in a way that resembles an artist's palette. The colourful displays in the windows of designer fashion shops and classy department stores demand attention and as night falls the waters of the canals and rivers sparkle reflecting the night sky.

Christmas starts and the New Year is welcomed by spectacular firework displays and throughout the festive period European Markets bring colour and inviting aromas to the streets.

Over the last twelve months I have spent many an evening photographing the city from a nocturnal perspective aiming to record not just the buildings and street scenes, but also the many events and activities that take place after dark that are missed by so many Mancunians.

In this album I have aimed to show Manchester illuminated in more ways than one. If when next in the city you are now tempted to stay a little later, do so – you will not be disappointed.

Mike Heath – February 2009

This nocturnal trip around Manchester starts with a look at the cathedral which for many years was somewhat detached from the main city centre. However, redevelopment of the surrounding area in the late nineties saw the creation of the 'Millennium Quarter' and reunited this magnificent building with its city.

As dusk descends upon the city the glazing that has allowed the light of day to penetrate the interiors of offices, apartments and shopping malls now performs a role reversal becoming a provider of much of the light that will illuminate the city centre during the hours of darkness.

Research tells me that it is built in the 'Perpendicular Gothic style' and
I can think of no better description when viewed from this angle.

At the northern tip of the city centre is Victoria Station, once one of the biggest passenger stations in Britain. The present Edwardian façade still carries an ornate iron and glass canopy bearing the names of original destinations which it served.

Internally the booking hall retains a Victorian elegance.

Thankfully the beautiful wall map painted on a tiled façade has been retained in all its glory by the entrance. It is interesting to note that the map only showed the railway network of the Lancashire and Yorkshire Railway omitting lines operated by rival railway companies.

In the 1980s the station was redeveloped to accommodate
the new Metrolink connection to Piccadilly Station.

Today the station largely serves destinations to the north and east of Manchester and forms a major interface with the Metrolink train which becomes a tramway through the city centre streets.

It is also the main terminus for the adjacent Manchester Evening News Arena, the construction of which obliterated the northern side of the station. The building itself is less than inspiring. . .

. . .but the spectacular shows put on by world famous groups certainly illuminate the interior.

Situated alongside Cathedral Gardens is Urbis. Opened in 2002 this ultra modern all glass structure houses a museum that offers a varied and ever-changing series of exhibitions and high tech displays exploring urban life in a modern city.

It also provides a home for Manchester's own TV channel – Channel M.

Once renowned as the largest newspaper office complex in the world, the Printworks produced its last paper in 1986 one year after the tycoon Robert Maxwell had purchased the plant! (He also renamed it Maxwell house – he must have liked coffee!!)

After 10 years of neglect, and the bombing, it was bought by a Birmingham-based development company who have refurbished it behind the original façade into a popular entertainment centre with a cinema, night clubs, bars and coffee shops.

Internally there are many retained features as reminders of former glories.

New Year's Eve revellers congregate below the wall of colour above the rear Dantzic Street entrance.

triangle
triangle
Shopping Centre
triangle
Shopping Centre
O'NEILL
adidas
CORN & PRODUCE EXCHANGE
SALE
70%
OFF

Left:
Those seeking the thoughts behind the name adorning the former Corn Exchange building need look no further than the shape of the site on which the structure was built between 1897 and 1903.

Right:
The Exchange ceased trading in the sixties and until becoming one of the major casualties of the1996 IRA bombing had been a temporary home to the then new Royal Exchange Theatre Company before being taken over by a thriving flea market. Here books, records and second hand clothes could be purchased and tarot cards readers and New Age mystics plied their trade. Small firms involved in everything from poetry publishing to private detective work could be found along the corridors of the upper floors.

Badly damaged by the bombing the Exchange
has since been rebuilt as a shopping mall.

Alongside the Triangle is Exchange Square the focal point for most of Manchester's redevelopment since the devastation of the blast.

Above:
The Manchester Wheel is similar to the London Eye but smaller and transportable, and as such is temporary. It offers tourists and shoppers a unique view across the roof tops. . .

Right:
. . .and photographers the opportunity to record movement using time exposure.

ARNDALE

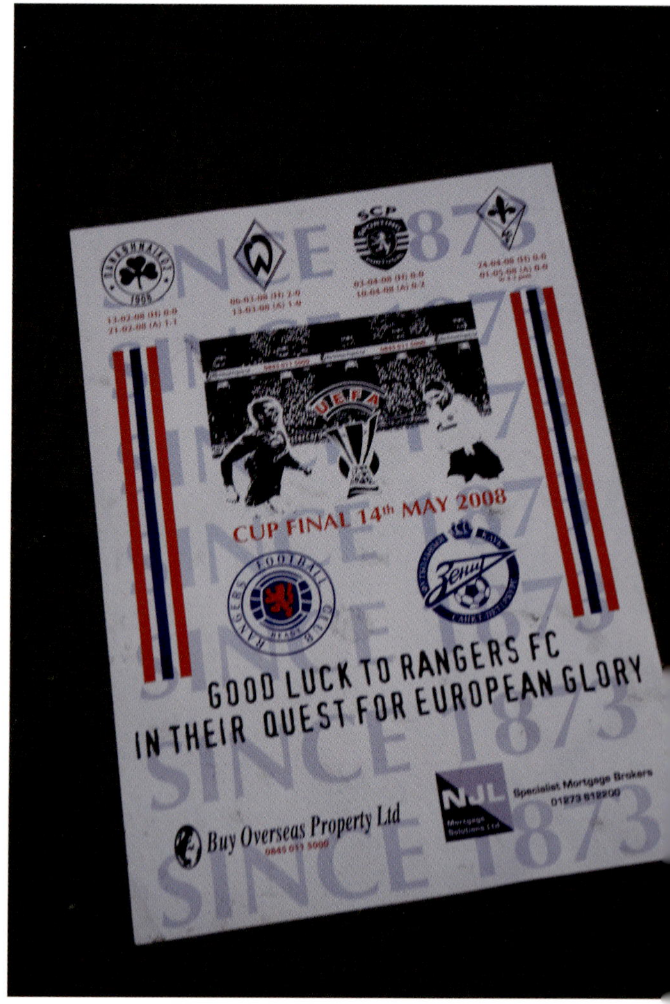

In May 2008, like much of the city, the square was taken over by Glasgow Rangers fans who had ventured south to support their team in the EUFA Cup Final being played at the City of Manchester Stadium. Large screens had been erected in various locations to cater for the ticketless hordes.

As the evening turned into night all eyes were on the big screen. With the match well underway a good time was had by all but the result did not match the mood!
(The morning after saw a thick carpet of litter welcome commuters trying to get to their place of work.)

Just off Exchange Square are the Old Wellington Inn and Sinclair's Oyster Bar. As part of the rebuilding programme these two historic pubs were dismantled and relocated alongside the square.

Exchange Square and
New Cathedral Street are now
home to some of the biggest
names in fashion.

Manchester was the location where Marks and Spencer set up their first shop and today the totally rebuilt flagship store dominates lower Market Street.

When opened in 1979 the original Arndale Centre was the largest covered town shopping centre in Europe. The centre has more recently been modernised with a new glass and steel entrance to Exchange Square and bridge across Market Street.

Above:
The view from Market Street itself.

Right:
Deansgate is Manchester's longest street and runs rigidly straight north–south. This view is taken from the 23rd floor of the North West's tallest building, Beetham Tower, located at the southern end of the street at its junction with Great Bridgewater Street.

GREAT NORTHERN RAILWAY COM

Above:
Along its length are many elegant buildings.

Right:
There cannot be many pubs quainter than the Sawyers Arms found at the junction with Quay Street. With its Victorian exterior consisting of maroon and cream tiling this building is reputed to have the longest running continuous public house licence in Manchester and is unique in retaining its original name since records began in 1734.

SAWYERS ARMS HOTEL
FANTASY BAR
SAWYERS ARMS
PUB & DINING
WELCOME TO THE
SAWYERS ARMS

Built 1890–99, by Enriqueta Augusta Rylands as a memorial to her cotton magnate husband the cathedral-like John Rylands Library at the junction with Wood Street, houses one of the world's greatest collection of theological books and manuscripts.

This office building, a former Congregational Church House dating from 1909–11, is dramatically lit and stands out on the west side of the street.

Linking Deansgate with St Ann's Square is Barton Arcade. A magnificent three storey glass and iron shopping arcade which boasts three tiers of balconies with ornamental balustrades and mahogany handrails. The whole building is topped by two glass domes.

St Ann's Square is one of the city's oldest and most distinguished squares. Known in the main as a high class shopping area it is actually dominated by St Ann's Church which dates from 1712. It is said that the church tower marks the exact centre of the City of Manchester. The statue depicts Richard Cobden.

Some of its distinguished round arched windows house beautiful stained glass which during the day would not attract a glance by passers-by.

Standing proud in the centre of the square is the Boer War Memorial, a rifleman protecting his wounded comrade.

Dominating the southern edge of the square is the Royal Exchange building, formerly the historic cotton exchange the trading floor of which was reputed to be 'the biggest room in the world'. This 'room' now houses The Royal Exchange Theatre which is the world's largest theatre in-the-round with seating for up to 800 people.

Alongside the theatre entrance is a shopping arcade that links St Ann's Square with Cross Street, seen here all dressed up for Christmas.

habitat

Above:
St Ann's Passage leads through to King Street.

Left:
St Ann Street leads back to Deansgate opposite the old established and prestigious Kendals Department Store. Its Art Deco façade is listed as a building of architectural merit.

King Street is home to Manchester's most exclusive shops
housed in antiquated looking buildings. The mock
Tudor half timbering actually dates from 1902.

Spinningfields is a newly developed quarter bounded by Deansgate, Bridge Street, Quay Street and the River Irwell.

The area combines retail, leisure, business . . .

. . . and public open spaces.

Among the most unusual buildings within the area are the new Magistrates Courts which have been likened to an open filing cabinet or a giant Jenga game! (I do like the 'Doves of Peace' statue by the entrance.)

The River Irwell is the natural boundary that separates Manchester from Salford. This view west is from the Albert Bridge on Bridge Street.

To the east is Trinity Bridge, a footbridge linking St Mary's Parsonage with Salford's Chapel Wharf. The curved building is the Lowry Hotel. I wonder how many people walking over Albert Bridge are aware of the lovely views available from above the parapet.

The area still retains a few elegant old buildings including the 'Opera House', on Quay Street, which originally opened as the 'New Theatre' on Boxing Day in 1912. It has always been a celebrated theatre and in its time has put on shows featuring great actors such as Sir John Geilgud and Peter Ustinov to name just two. It also carries an identification sign in Lancashire dialect!

Above:
The Lock-keeper's Cottage was apparently built at an angle so that the lock-keeper had a clear view of the Bridgewater Canal basin and along the Rochdale Canal.

Left:
Castlefield was the Roman birthplace of Manchester and was to become by the mid-nineteenth century the industrial hub of the city with its network of roads, rivers, canals and railways. The area was designated as Britain's first Urban Heritage Park containing a wealth of industrial heritage centred between railway viaducts, canal systems and warehouses, many of which have been converted to modern use. Duke's Lock marks the junction of the Rochdale and Bridgewater Canals.

In the midst of all the Victorian splendour is the 'new' Merchants Bridge. This tubular steel structure, erected in 1996, crosses the canal in a curving sweep and makes an interesting contrast with the cobbled towpath beneath it.

Today the view from Duke's Lock up the Rochdale Canal is dominated by Beetham Tower. At 171 metres tall with 48 storeys this is one of the tallest mixed-use buildings in Britain. The tower includes over 200 apartments atop a five-star hotel. Note the step in the structure where the upper floors are built out four metres wider than the lower floors. The 'aerial' photographs contained within these pages were taken from the hotel's panoramic Lounge Bar on the 23rd floor at the 'step'.

Above:
Manchester's transport network encompassed within one photograph. The mainline railway is represented by Deansgate Station with its tubular link to the Metrolink Station across Whitworth Street and the Rochdale Canal below. Deansgate sweeps in bottom right, heading out of the city as Chester Road from the junction.

Left:
The skewed bridge that carries the railway across the Rochdale Canal is just one of many elegant Victorian feats of engineering that have stood the test of time in this area.

Above:
There is even a bicycle outside the railway station!

Right:
Alongside Whitworth Street, beneath the Metrolink are Deansgate Locks, where the railway arches have been converted to bars and bistros.

This is one of the most popular night spots of the city. (Photo Karl Heath)

The Rochdale Canal runs parallel to Whitworth Street as it skirts the southern edge of the city's Conference Quarter, Peter's Fields.

The towpath clearly signposted for pedestrians.(Main Photo Karl Heath)

Pride of place in the area goes to the GMEX Exhibition Centre
and the equally impressive Bridgewater Hall.

The GMEX exhibition centre, now rebranded as Manchester Central, started life in 1880 as Manchester's Central Station and served as a major railway terminus until closure in 1969. Now the single span roof provides an undivided 7,500sq.m. exhibition space which can also serve as a sporting or concert venue.

Completed in 1996 the Bridgewater Hall is reputed to be one of the most acoustically superior classical music venues in the world. To this end the building is mounted on a system of giant foundation 'springs' to isolate it from the vibrations and noise from passing traffic.

Above:
The hall is home to both the Hallé and BBC Philharmonic Orchestras.

Right:
Alongside is a purpose-built basin linked to the nearby Rochdale Canal.
Colourful barges can often be seen moored here.

The Hallé Orchestra's former base was the Free Trade Hall in Peter Street. A formidable building to which these photographs do not really do justice. Now forming part of a large hotel, the halls that have stood on this site over the years have been the setting for everything from political events to rock concerts. I understand that the likes of Gladstone, Disraeli, Lloyd George and Churchill have in the past bellowed their beliefs to the rafters. My own recollections include Paul McCartney and Wings, a foot stomping evening with Roy Wood's Wizzard and Elton John dancing on his piano!

Next door is the impressive Theatre Royal, which dates from 1845, and is the city's oldest surviving theatre though now in use as a night club.

GREAT NORTHERN RAILWAY COMPANY'S

Above:
It is difficult to visualise nowadays but it provided an interchange between the road, rail and canal networks in Manchester.

Left:
This Grade 2 listed warehouse, which still boldly proclaims its lineage in large white letters was built in 1898 and at the time was at the forefront of freight transportation.

There was a tunnel beneath connected to the Manchester & Salford Canal junction and a specially built viaduct linked its huge marshalling yard with the Central Station (now GMEX). Goods were raised and lowered hydraulically. Ignominiously the building spent many years as a car park but has more recently been brought back to life following full restoration adding shopping and leisure facilities.

The whole Peter Street frontage has been opened out to create a public square with several cafés and bars creating a colourful centrepiece. The 'Albert Hall' in the background has no connection with its London namesake. Built in 1910 this former Wesleyan Mission Hall lay dormant for over a decade after closure in 1971 until renovation as a bar.

Above:
The Midland Hotel occupies a prime location on Peter Street and first opened in 1903 having been built by the Midland Railway Company.

Right:
An immense building, it offers over 300 ensuite bedrooms and 14 luxury suites with an exterior clad in red brick, polished granite and pink and brown terracotta. Its claim to fame being the location for the meeting of Mr Rolls and Mr Royce, leading to the formation of their famous motor company.

The hotel itself is one of Manchester's premier venues for meetings and conferences and in 2008 in conjunction with the adjacent G-Mex centre hosted the Labour Party Conference with all its associated street furniture…

...that formed a ring of steel around the whole area. There were also hundreds of policemen busily patrolling the streets but most of them were able to spare me a few moments to have a look at the photographs I had taken!!

Across from the hotel is the Central Library. Construction of this purpose-built library commenced in 1930 and King George V attended the grand opening four years later. The classical exterior style disguises the fact that it was built around a 'modern' steel frame.

St Peter's Square takes its name from the church that stood here from 1788 to 1907.
The cenotaph was erected in 1924 and is a close replica of that which stands in London's Whitehall.

There are more monuments in front of the Town Hall in Albert Square. The Jubilee Fountain, the statue of John Bright and the Albert Memorial itself, which was funded by public subscription as the nation mourned Victoria's Prince Consort.

The Jubilee Fountain was commissioned for the Diamond Jubilee of Queen Victoria and completed well in time for the celebrations in 1897. Having spent 30 years in the square it was moved to Heaton Park where it languished for 70 years before returning, fully restored, to the city centre in 1997.

Left:
Oxford Street marks the eastern edge of the 'Peter's Fields' area and the dominant tower of the former Refuge Assurance headquarters building is one of the best known landmarks.
(Photo Karl Heath)

Right:
The brick and terracotta building, opened in 1910, is Grade 2 listed and was converted into a hotel in 1996.
(Photo Karl Heath)

REFUGE ASSURANCE CO.
Appearing Here..
CHRISTMAS PARTY TIME
BEATLES
Saturday 20th December 2008
Appearing Here..
New Year's Eve Ball
01706 650515
www.ticketweb.co.uk
REFUGE ASSURANCE CO.

The Palace Theatre made its grand opening in 1891. The first performance was the ballet 'Cleopatra' viewed by a full house. Unfortunately, subsequent 'highbrow' productions did not attract the same audience numbers and in order to make ends meet the scope of their repertoire was broadened to include the more popular performers of the day. The television revolution of the sixties and seventies threatened its future as entertainment at home became the order of the day, but following intervention by the Arts Council in the eighties, and after considerable internal refurbishment it is now one of the best equipped and most popular theatres outside London.

Believe it or not this former underground public convenience is now a thriving, if intimate, bar. The sound of music and merriment now drifts from this hole in the ground just off Oxford Street. A far cry from what may have drifted from below before!

Having passed beneath Oxford Street the Rochdale Canal continues in a claustrophobic passage between buildings old and new.

However, once Princess Street is passed the cityscape opens out along Canal Street, an area that suffered greatly as a result of the decline of the cotton industry leaving many derelict warehouses.

It has now been transformed into a centrepiece of trendy cafés, bars and clubs and is the focus of Manchester's famous Gay Village.

Manchester Pride is the annual lesbian, gay, bisexual and transgender festival that provides a nonstop programme of music, arts, entertainment and of course partying. The culmination of the event is centred on Sackville Park where following an evening of entertainment and fireworks. . .

. . .a candle lit vigil is held to remember those whose lives have been affected by HIV. All in the park stand in quiet reflection in the flickering candlelight.

The candles are then lovingly placed around the bases of the trees (pre-protected) and the park vacated to let the partying continue. There is a truly magical and moving atmosphere on the evening and being there was a very emotional experience.

For most rail passengers arriving at Manchester, Piccadilly Station is their first taste of the city. The first station opened here in 1842.

The original iron sheds with their decorative cast iron columns date from the 1880s when the station was the terminus for the Manchester and Birmingham line.

The station now serves all destinations south via inter-city and local cross-country routes with modern technology advising travellers of arrivals, departures and the occasional delay!

The main station buildings were rebuilt in 1969 and subsequently remodelled for the 2002 Commonwealth Games.

More recent development along London Road has seen the construction of a footbridge linking the station with a new hotel and car park.

With congestion charges vetoed, parking space within the city is at a premium and there are many innovative ideas to overcome the problem. I just managed to get this shot before a Traffic Warden arrived with a ladder.

FIRE STATION
BUS STOP

Above:
Opposite the station approach is the Malmaison Hotel which is attached to and incorporates the former Joshua Hoyle Warehouse which was built in 1904.

Left:
Across from the station is the ornate terracotta London Road fire station. This incredible structure, built 1904–06, occupies a triangular plot and has a central courtyard with a series of balconies. It provided working and living quarters for around forty firemen and their families and had its own library, stables, bank and gymnasium. Abandoned in the 1980s, but thankfully Grade 2 listed, this building is currently undergoing refurbishment work.

Piccadilly is the main gateway into Manchester for those arriving by train and for many years Piccadilly Gardens provided a refuge from the hurly burly of traffic , work and shopping with its well tended flower beds and many park benches. In the mid1960s the Piccadilly Plaza complex was built on land reclaimed from the gardens. The 1990s saw the introduction of the Metrolink system which further reduced the recreational area.

More recently the southern end was sold and an office block developed.

The ‘gardens’ of today have been described as a “shabby square of muddy grass and play fountains flanked by an awkward concrete wall, bus station, tram lines and ugly office block”.

Knowing what was there before I find it difficult to argue against this opinion but the area does have a certain attractiveness after dark.

Just off Piccadilly and Market Street is 'The Shakespeare' public house. This has a fascinating history as in the 1920s the complete pub was moved from Chester where it had been known as the 'Shambles'.

It retains the black and white Tudor façade and internally old wooden floors and oak beams.

Manchester's development as a major centre for the textile and cotton industry meant that by the mid 1800s there was a large amount of money flowing around the city. The Bank of Manchester was the first true bank, established in 1829, and many others soon followed as the area of Spring Gardens, Fountain Street and King Street became the city's banking centre. Many fine buildings sprang up to house these institutions and now most have been converted, many to cater for the public's leisure requirements. One such conversion has seen the former Parr's Bank, with its opulent banking hall, become the 'Athenaeum' wine bar-café.

The Manchester Art Gallery, on Mosley Street, is housed in what was originally the home of the Manchester Institution for the Promotion of Science, Literature and the Arts constructed 1827–35. Its owners offered it to the Corporation for free, in 1882, providing that councillors spent £2000 per year for twenty years on new works of art. This set the foundation for what has become the country's best collection of Pre-Raphaelite paintings.

The restaurants and ethnic stores that make up Chinatown occupy the old Victorian cotton warehouses that could have been demolished had council plans for the area in the 1960s come to fruition. That they did not allowed Chinese restaurateurs to take over the lower floors of the buildings and by the 1970s it was clear that a new Chinatown was emerging.

The Chinese Imperial Arch, built by Chinese craft workers in 1987 to a traditional design straddles Faulkner Street and is the focal point for the area particularly during the Chinese New Year celebrations when thousands of Mancunians descend upon the area.

During the festival the streets are lined with stalls, sideshows and street theatre offering everything from quiet reflection and worship to moving pictures projected onto a bare wall. . .

. . .and no Chinese celebration would be complete without a spectacular firework display.

The Rochdale Canal having passed through the Gay Village disappears under Piccadilly and Dale Street to emerge in an area of substantial redevelopment alongside Ducie Street.

Above:
We now move away from the city centre to what, for some unknown reason, most sports fans all over the world think of first when Manchester is mentioned.

Right:
Match night at Old Trafford where the 'reds' were playing my own team, the valiant Bolton Wanderers from just up the road.

MANCHESTER UNITED

'The Theatre of Dreams'? (Unfortunately betwixt taking the last photograph and this one from Salford Quays, we were down two goals to nil!)

A little further afield is that which most sports fans' wives think of first when descending on Manchester , The Trafford Centre. This opened in 1998 and was then, and may still be, the largest shopping and leisure complex in Europe. The main entrance is a little understated . . .

. . .and there was no let up in the extravagance with the design of the most recent extension, Barton Square.

As the name suggests Salford Quays is not actually in the City of Manchester but is inextricably linked as this major regeneration project covers the area which in its previous life was the bustling Port of Manchester, better known as Manchester Docks. In the photograph from left to right is the Lowry Footbridge spanning the Manchester Ship Canal, the Lowry Centre and the Lowry Outlet Shopping Mall.

The stunning Lowry Centre was built in 2000 and houses two theatres and brings fine examples of contemporary art to its galleries. It is also home to the largest Lowry collection in the world.

The NV Buildings occupy the prime location by Huron Basin. These impressive sail shaped apartment buildings typify the regeneration and its desirability as a residential area.

Above:
Just further along the former No 9 Dock, now known as Erie Basin, is The Victoria. This landmark office building utilises water from the dock in its air conditioning system which is filtered then returned to the basin.

Right:
The Mariners Canal, opened by the Duke of York in 1989, was built to link the former No 9 and 8 Docks (Erie and Ontario Basins). The footbridge in the centre is marked 'Grain Wharf' in deference to No 9 Dock where Canadian and American ships would unload their grain cargoes. It is worth noting that the names used in the Quays reflect the strong trading links the docks had with North America. (Photo Karl Heath)

The Detroit Bridge was formerly a twin-tracked railway bridge that linked the extensive dock-side railway system with Trafford Park across the Ship Canal. It was erected in 1942 to replace the original single track bridge. The whole structure had to be lowered onto pontoons and floated down the canal to its present position.

An interesting comparison between the basically Victorian designed 'Detroit Bridge' and the modern 'Lowry Footbridge' which is equally remarkable. The four giant piers each winch the deck high in the air to allow large ships to pass beneath and into the old dock area. (Photos Karl Heath)

Not an area that stays still, the Quays is now to become home to the UK's first Media City that will eventually cover two hundred acres of land. The intention is to develop a thriving media hub with a relocated BBC at its centre but also providing a base for other media and creative industries.

Moving back across the city and the great local football divide to the home of Manchester City. The City of Manchester Stadium, also known as Eastlands, became home to the football team at the beginning of the season in August 2003. Originally it had been built to host the 2002 Commonwealth Games and subsequently further developed to allow the 'Blues' to inherit it to replace their former home at Maine Road in the Moss Side district.

MANCHESTER CITY
FOOTBALL CLUB

MANCHESTER CITY
FOOTBALL CLUB

Taking pride of place by the stadium is Britain's tallest sculpture 'The B of the Bang'. This was commissioned to mark the success of the 2002 Commonwealth Games and the name is inspired by Olympic Gold medallist Linford Christie who has said that he started each race on the 'B' of the Bang of the starting pistol.

Unfortunately this magnificent structure has already had a chequered past and at the time of writing an uncertain future. Only two weeks after Linford Christie had unveiled it in January 2005 spikes began to drop off as it swayed in the wind and others have since been removed following detection of more defects. With typical northern humour locals have nick-named it Kerplunk although I prefer 'C' of the Clang! (Photos Karl Heath)

For the big Christmas lights switch-on all eyes are on the Town Hall as thousands of people descend on Albert Square. This neo-Gothic building was opened in1877 and is notable for its 85metre-high clock tower and intricate stone masonry details. There are also statues of prominent Mancunians along the façade at first floor level.

Whilst all eyes are towards the building its detail and history are of no relevance as the crowd are treated to an evening of entertainment and a spectacular firework display to launch the festivities.

Albert Square, named after Queen Victoria's husband, is pedestrianised and is a traditional congregation space for announcements, fairs and of course the famous Christmas Markets.

It wouldn't be Manchester without cobbles and puddles

Considered to be amongst the best in Britain and Europe the markets transform the city centre with traditional wooden chalets filling the streets.

In 2008 the St Ann's Square Market had a German theme. . .

. . .whilst shoppers were entertained by the Sale Brass Band. Meanwhile a Charity Choir sang carols in front of the Town Hall and 'Buddy' entertained those in New Cathedral Street with his one man band.

In Spinningfields a very popular ice rink was constructed for the holiday period and skaters of all ages, and capabilities, spent many a happy hour clinging on to the perimeter rail!

All too soon Christmas is over and fireworks on the roof of the Arndale mark the dawn of a New Year and bring to a conclusion this look around Manchester at night.

This particular book project, a departure from my usual railway-based subject, has been a thoroughly enjoyable experience and I would like to place on record my thanks to Halsgrove for giving me the opportunity to spread my photographic wings. I should also acknowledge the management and staff of the Manchester Hilton Hotel for allowing me to roam freely around their Cloud 23 Bar late one winter's afternoon. The view from there is exhilarating.